It's Dark in Here: Essays about Life with Depression

By Dr. Tiffany Wicks

Acknowledgments

To all those who struggle to function day to day, to be present, to stay alive…I see you. You are not alone even in the loneliest of moments. Thank you for choosing to stay alive every day.

To my husband, Donovan... Thank you for helping me live and helping me find hope when I can't find it. And thank you for loving me for who I am beyond my diagnoses. I love you forever.

To my kids. I hope you still feel loved, heard, and validated in spite of my inability to consistently be well. I hope I can normalize that mental illness does not define you, but just a part of who you are.

To my friends, thank you. Thank you for letting me be vulnerable and not placing conditions of wellness on our friendship. You are my chosen family and I'm honored to have you in my life.

Dedication

For Ali and Nancy.

It's Dark in Here
A Poem by Shel Silverstein

I am writing these poems

From inside a lion,

And it's rather dark in here.

So please excuse the handwriting

Which may not be too clear.

But this afternoon by the lion's cage

I'm afraid I got too near.

And I'm writing these lines

From inside a lion,

And it's rather dark in here.

Introduction

I have struggled with chronic depression since I was 15 years old. However, I didn't start therapy until I was 19, and didn't get medication until I was 22. I have been diagnosed with major depressive disorder (MDD), generalized anxiety disorder (GAD), seasonal affective disorder (SAD), and attention deficit and hyperactivity disorder (ADHD). But this doesn't define me.

I am a therapist, business owner, wife and mom. No matter what titles I hold, I struggle daily to function and accomplish even the smallest of tasks. It often takes me a long time to achieve my goals. I may look good on paper, but few people know the battle to get there.

The stigma of mental illness and receiving help often prevents us from talking about what we need from friends and family to survive. Coping with depression, anxiety, and other diagnoses should be a part of everyday conversations so we can normalize that mental illness is not who we are but only a part of us. Even though 1 in 4 people struggle in some way, our society is still battling to normalize mental illness.

My hope is that as you read these essays you feel seen and heard. If you struggle, you can probably relate to the days you are just trying to live, and the days you can celebrate pulling yourself out of the hole. And for many of us, we just celebrate the days we got of bed, showered, or went to work despite the darkness that looms. I wrote these essays throughout my years of living with chronic mental illness to help myself stay alive. Now I want to share them with you to remind you that you are not alone.

I encourage you to seek the support you need for you. This may look like therapy, medication, friendship, or support groups. Whatever you choose has to be right for you, but don't keep going alone. I find that on my darkest days that no matter how hard I try to isolate, my team rallies around me and it eventually helps me heal.

I hope from reading, you are encouraged not to stay in the darkness. You are not your diagnosis. You matter and deserve to survive and thrive.

If you are experiencing a mental health crisis, please reach out for help.

National Suicide Hotline: 1800-273-8255

The GLBT National Hotline: 1888- 843-4564

Trans Lifeline: 1877-565-8860

Perinatal Help Line: 1800-944-4773

Part 1: Drowning

SOS

I'm literally trying to stay alive. Every minute I do not put a gun to my head is a win. It's awful wanting to die all the time. I'm sick of being depressed. Every day I'm trying to will myself to be productive, but I can't do it. I always hope a run or work out would do me good, but I genuinely just don't have it in me. I need a change to believe there is a good in the world and not just coincidence. I am tired of spinning my wheels. I have potential and skills, but I can't function a full day without an anxiety or panic attack or a major depressive episode. I need so much help. I need to not want to die. I'm tired and I try so hard to not be angry because I'm not well. I know other people have it worse than me. However, this is my reality and I feel what I feel. I'm still miserable and hate my life every day.

I can't keep going like this.

I know you read this. I know you hear me.

PLEASE HEAR ME!!!

PLEASE DO SOMETHING!!!

I need a miracle. To save my life. I don't want to die but I sure as hell don't want to live like this.

The Darkness Masked

The darkness of depression comes in waves, but there's always a shade of grey present. When life is light gray, I am able to move through different spaces with less stress to find a way to put a smile on my face. It is the easiest of the hard days. It's the days when medication works, when I see my therapist. I live for the light gray days. But even though those days occur in large chunks which allows me to stay alive, to maintain employment, and to function, the darkness lurks.

I can only feel everything turn to black as I quickly move from hopeful to depressed. I sit numb to the world around me as I lay in bed willing myself to utilize hygiene products or drink enough water to stay hydrated. I lay catatonic in the heaviness of sadness, grief, loneliness. My mind occasionally rumbles through thoughts but there is no hopefulness. They are thoughts of pain, sadness, doom. I cannot convince myself my past accomplishments will lead to success again. I failed at everything and there is no chance for success. Every now and then I have the fleeting thought to reach for help, but it only pops up following the thought of dying. I cannot see the light, it doesn't exist. I continue my stillness in bed until I hear the voices of others nearing.

As my partner approaches, his soft voice offers to get me active, to help make me better. While the attempt is nice in theory, obligation to movement and feeling better is as heavy as my thoughts. How am I supposed to be active in the dark? And then the second voice enters. Her little stature and large smile remind me I'm needed. Not just from her, but I am needed because I am a helper in profession and in character. I empathize and absorb the darkness from others to keep them from hurting the way I do only to feel more darkness that I cannot manage. As I remember, she requests to go outside.

The darkness is still so halting, but it's time. I put on my mask to hide my pain and head out the door.

With my mask, I can move through the day just as if it's light gray. I function, I help, and I meet the needs of others without missing a beat. I am "on" because others expect me to be. On the darkest of days, I use my mask to forget and ignore, which is my best friend and worst enemy. She asks me once again to go play. She is so little and cannot do for herself what those older than her can. My role is to sustain her life and health and make her feel safe. I put on my mask, go outside, and play for her to be none the wiser. She needs me, so I meet her needs. I keep my mask on to network, to work, and to fulfill my various roles. They hurt too and they depend on me to help alleviate their pain and turmoil and stress. Life is hectic and heavy for them and I exist to lighten the load. I work hard so they don't hurt as much. They need me, so I meet their needs.

At the end of the day, I try to persuade myself that I was around enough people not to feel alone. I lie to myself and say I did enough to feel satisfied. The darkness creeps as I lie, knowing I can't maintain my false sense of self. The moment I arrive home, the quiet comes. The mask falls even though I wish I could keep it on until I fall asleep. The darkness is still there as if it was taunting me all along to keep its promise to appear again.

I am once again consumed with self-loathing hopelessness that reminds me of the lies I told today to mask all my pain to those around me. I overanalyze what I did wrong, the stupid things I said, the feigned confidence that took every ounce of my energy. There is so much hate in the darkness. I will myself to sleep to keep my thoughts at bay for a few hours so I can rest my mind, my hate, my fears. My dreams don't soothe me, but they don't haunt me. I just need a few hours in literal darkness as a break from my darkness.

What seems like minutes is apparently hours. I wake up, consciously reminded of the hurts and emotional pain that plagues me. I turn to my phone to texts and messages. They need me. A few minutes later, her bright and smiling face enters my room. She needs me. I take a deep breath, throw off the covers, and put on my mask to face a new day. Someone needs me, and me and my mask will meet those needs.

A Letter to Me

Dear You,

Sometimes it's hard to see you because the place you're in is so dark and hidden and you don't let anyone in, not even yourself. You want to die, and while that's not the best option, it's going to be hard to convince you otherwise. If you told anyone, they would try and guilt you out of it. You know those friends who will remind you that you have a daughter and a husband that love you and would be sad without you. But all you want is someone to stop looking at you as responsible to someone else and actually talk to you. You want them to see how much you're hurting and take it away. You didn't understand why your body and now your mind has failed you, but now that it has, you're done. You didn't ask for this. No one does. But I want to tell you what no one else will. You matter.

You. You as an individual matter. I see how much hurt you've endured, but I've seen how long you've chosen to stay. That matters too. As much as you want to die to make the pain go away, you also want to live. You want to see your baby girl grow strong and become an independent thinker and self-starter like you want to raise her to be. Living for her is not enough though. It might keep you another day or maybe even another week, but you have to live for you. I know were meant for greatness. You have so many ideas and dreams and you want to be even more than you've already become. You don't see it now, but who you are and what you do make an impact. Whether you see it today or not, that impact is immediate for the people around you, for your co-workers, for your partner, and for the strangers you meet every day. Your ability to smile through the pain doesn't help you, but your still holds a power that you can tap into once again.

So why stay here? The world is not kind, and often is full of shame for struggling. You have these expectations for yourself that don't fit what you can do and be right now. That's why you're suffering. I think it's more about permission to fail than pushing through to the next day. How do you forgive yourself for not being the mom society expects you to be? There's no one answer for this. Acceptance is daily. It's celebrating the small things you did right and remembering that the things you did wrong can always be better tomorrow. Acceptance is the constant reminder that you will never be everything to everyone. Acceptance is setting boundaries to not give 100% to everything when you only have 15% of you to give. It's also the ability to say when you can no longer function at 15% and need more support than you're willing to admit now.

It's okay to not be okay. But it's what you do with not being okay that matters. Dying would make the pain go away for you, but it makes you go away too. I have a feeling there's some fight left in you to stay here. It's okay to ask for help. Counselors seem out of reach or out of touch because of your previous experiences or the judgments you think those therapists will have about you. The question you have to ask yourself is, "Is it worth continuing on alone and feeling like death is my only option?" If the answer is no, the next part is not easy. You have to take the risk of telling someone about your deep pain. Be honest. Choose someone who will open their arms instead of panic. Choose someone who can make the call for mental health support with you so you're not alone as you talk to a stranger about feeling like this. Choose people who you need right now more than they need you, so you step onto a new road of healing instead of the painful road you currently walk. When you make these hard and painful steps, you choose yourself. You are making the conscious decision to let others in and considering staying not just one more day, but a lifetime. This new path is not just based on survival, but it's the embrace of hope and moving forward. It's the vulnerability of allowing people to see you as you wanted them to always see you. It might not be the best of circumstances to be seen, but it's out there and the blank slate of feeling so empty only lends itself to be written.

So as you sit there in your own hell, just know that I see you. It's not okay now, but it can be. You don't always have to hide in the darkness, but you have to do it for you. Stay for you so it's not just temporary and it's not because you're somebody's someone. If you're willing, take the chance to explore that life could be beyond good and actually be great for you and those who you love and care for.

I hope you stay. I see and feel that small ounce of life left and I'm hoping you feel it too. And when you stay, live. You deserve more than what you've had before, but facing death at rock bottom means there's a chance it's better tomorrow than what it was today. You matter to me. And I hope you live.

Part 2: Functioning and Connecting

Just Keep Swimming

Do you remember "Finding Nemo"? Do you remember Dory who says "Just Keep Swimming" and stayed positive all the time? While I love that movie so much, that phrase does not work for someone buried in the thick of depression. And yet, I feel like we HAVE to keep swimming, and it sucks.

Recently I was going through one of my longest bouts of depression that I've experienced. I couldn't get myself out of the hole of sadness, numbness, and just an all-around low. So I decided to fight my fears and be open about my struggles so other people feel free to be open about their struggles. However, I neglected to remind myself that most people who don't deal with mental illness on a daily basis or avoid it with negative coping do not know what to say to someone in the thick of their struggle. So a friend sent me a gif and told me to "Just keep swimming". I almost threw my phone across the room. It's the LAST thing I need. I've kept swimming because I must, because I'm a mom, because I run a business, because everyone needs something. But because I kept swimming, I am drowning from taking on everything for everyone and not able to pause to combat the oncoming wave of darkness in order to cope for myself and stay afloat. I can't keep swimming because I'm already drowning.

For the darker days, I'm not going to keep swimming. I can't play around and hope I come out of my depression while I keep doing the same things that are sinking me. I also don't answer to anyone else but me.

See Me

I don't write everything that I am actually feeling. I don't want you to see all of me. It's better to have the façade of managing my mental illness and my life than knowing how often I'm just a pile of goo trying to pick myself up off the floor.

I've said before it's easy for me to put up the wall and become someone that I'm not just to guard everything from everyone. It's terrifying for other people to know my strength AND my struggle because they might not want to stick around for the struggle. I have to censor myself to be closer to who I am on paper than who I am in reality.

When I get close with someone, I push them away in efforts to reject them before they reject me. I fear rejection. None of us like rejection, but once we've experienced it, we sometimes allow fear in that dictates our next relationships.

I want to know that no matter the health level of my emotional and mental state, the people I'm close with will never let me go. The only problem with that scenario is that if I don't let anyone in, I have essentially rejected myself.

I have lost hope for any opportunity to live a healthy life with people around me to love and be loved. There has to be a point where we have someone call our bluff.

I honestly would rather have someone be able to read between the lines and be there for me than me have to be "on" to meet the expectation of the me I want people to see.

If you have that one person you can trust, keep them. Show them everything. Let them show up for you. And when they do, don't question it. They have a choice, and they chose you. It's okay to accept the love they WANT to give.

Missed Call

Friend,

I'm sorry I missed your call. This week has been so crazy that I've been so caught up.

Actually that's not true. You see, the kids have so many activities and I don't like to be on the phone and drive.

No, that's not it either.

My phone has been so weird lately, and I've been missing calls without getting a notification.

Nope.

Okay. The truth is that I'm not well. I'm really depressed. I've been ignoring and not responding to your texts. I've been sending your calls to voicemail or waiting for it to stop ringing so you don't know that I'm actually avoiding your call.

Most days it's hard to even breathe let alone wake up, shower, be a real person. I just CANNOT talk on the phone. Part of me is scared you will hear how bad things are. The other part of me is scared you'll leave our friendship realizing how much support I need. Either way, it terrifies me for you to hear me.

I know we talk about deep topics, but I rarely tell you about my mental state. I think it's best we keep it that way. Even opening up to you takes energy I don't have.

I have this urge to say I'm sorry. I want to apologize for being like this. However, I'm not sure that's the right thing to do given that this is part of who I am. One day I will tell you everything. But today, maybe this week, I will just have to miss your call.

Love,

Me

Part 3: Parenting

A Very Dark Hole

First the first time in four years, I wanted to die today. It's almost noon and I'm still fighting those thoughts. I chose to write through them instead of let them linger. Depression is a deep dark hole that some people fall in and regardless of the existence of a dim flashlight, it seems the hole is too deep. Wanting to die and making a plan to die are two different things, but for today, I just wanted to die.

I know when it's dangerous and when I should call for help. Even when I don't want to do it, I do it anyway. Today was not the call for help day. It was just the hole. I woke up this morning not able to wake myself up enough to get out of bed. The only thing that really woke me was the fact that all I have done today is feed the baby and go back to sleep.

As usual, my loving husband starts to get up and get into "do stuff" mode as he calls it. However, he does it right after I sit down with the kids. I know for him it gives him a chance to have his arms free for a moment, but my brain says he's getting up to avoid me. That's the depression lie. *You're not wanted. You're a nuisance.* And for weeks now I feel like I am only useful as a food source for my son.

So he gets up and invites me to go to the store. This is his sweet attempt to get me out of the house and moving for the day. He knows. He sees me even when I am in deep denial that something is wrong. I say okay, but I knew I wasn't going to the store. I want to go back to bed. So I head upstairs while he is getting dressed and he valiantly tries to get me talking and interacting while I'm holding the baby. Attempt three. I love him for it, but the hole is dark. He asks again if I want to go to the store. I say no this time. He says he would be more than happy to take the kids if I want to rest more. I tell him I'm keeping the baby. Somehow, in all of this, the baby brings me a peace that I crave. Husband doesn't leave.

He's worried. As much as I know my husband loves me, I often feed into the lie that I need to apologize for my mental health issues. I'm sorry I'm depressed. I'm sorry I had a panic attack. I'm sorry I cry so much. I'm sorry I retreat. And all those apologies just pile onto the wanting to die feeling. There's a lie in there about no one wanting me and everything just putting up with me waiting for me to fix myself. I know in my head it's not true, but in the hole it's the only truth.

He leaves the room. I close the bedroom door. He comes back and asks if I could just tell him what's going on. In my head I'm screaming, "I WANT TO DIE". I fight it and nothing comes out. He leaves me be. I start sobbing. It's uncontrollable at this point. I'm grieving the fact that after my suicide attempt and my friend's attempt the same year, I have had minimal suicidal ideation. I have worked so hard for my mental health and know how I need to cope even on the hardest of days. I'm so proud of that, but here I am, feeling like I am a big giant burden and that life sucks too much. I feel like no one should have to deal with me and how hard it is to make me feel better. Again, in my head I KNOW it's a lie, but that hole just gets darker.

I look at my son and beg God for him to smile. Maybe if he smiles at me, I can know for a moment I'm loved. Maybe I can fight the idea that my husband should find a wife that isn't mentally ill and beats herself up about being mentally ill because she's a therapist. Maybe I can find the strength to find and follow a dim light that leads me out of the dark hole. Maybe.

He smiles.

I'd like to finish this story and tell you I'm fine and everything is good now. I can't do that. Do I want to die at this current moment while writing this? No. Did saying these things without shame help me? Yes. But I'm not much better today and I might actually go back to napping once again. Right now, I'm holding my son tight and taking in all the oxytocin our bond brings. I'm planning to tell my husband I'm not okay, and I don't know what I need. But I know that the hole doesn't get less dark if we stay silent. I have to say something to someone otherwise the hole gets dark again. When I say something, someone is usually there with a flashlight or a ladder. When I say something, it takes the power out of the lie. And I remember they are just that…LIES. So that's my plan because I never want to attempt suicide again and I worked too damn hard to lose me again. It's not to say I won't have days where I'm lost. But I want there to be more days where I'm found.

May you be found today.

Mentally Ill Mom

Over the weekend I was reflecting on why it takes so long to do pretty much any big project. I've dropped so many projects, tasks, and to-do lists because it felt so heavy. But why?

Well, even though "life" happens, the truth is that I'm mentally ill. I have major depressive disorder and generalized anxiety. It makes little moments big, and big moments almost unbearable. I've done meds, no meds, different meds, therapy, all of it. I can't live without meds because I truly have a chemical imbalance. This sucks! I have things to do and dreams to chase but every few weeks or months I get in such a dark place that make the smallest of tasks impossible to accomplish.

On top of the stuff, I have to parent. And parenting two small children while trying to stay mentally stable SUUUCCKKSSS. I can either be a mom or I can prioritize my health. Doing both gives me anxiety and doing neither makes me depressed. It's so hard to manage who I want to be with the situation I am in now. I always have something to do for someone and I don't sleep normal hours. It is a daily battle to be mentally ill and productive.

But that's mental illness. Where function isn't the same as the ideas. I fight it. Every. Single. Day. And it's hard, and I often fail. And my husband often picks up the pieces because he can sometimes see the dark cloud coming before I do.

If you suffer from chronic mental illness, applaud EVERY accomplishment. You took a shower today? Hell yes. You parented? Yes! You marked off one thing that to do list? Go you!!

On paper I might look like a badass at times, but no one knows how long and hard I worked to finish the task. Secretly, my daily applause goes to showering and not staying in bed until noon. Each day is a different challenge. But I'll be damned if I don't keep fighting.

Panic and Parenting

It was just another weekday morning when I had my first anxiety attack in front of my toddler. I was on my way to work and getting my daughter ready for school. As always, my daughter was running around the house, refusing to get dressed. I still had to finish styling my hair, packing lunches and get my work bag ready for the day. It was too much.

I dropped the knife that I was using to spread the mayonnaise. My dogs started barking when they heard another dog being walked in the neighborhood. There was now 15 minutes to get out the door and I could feel time ticking. At this point, I'm yelling through the house, trying to find my daughter, begging her to ditch her pajamas. She refused. Ten minutes left. She was screaming and trying to run while I wrestled to at least get a new shirt over her head. She wriggled away. I just couldn't do it anymore! My heart started racing. Pounding. It was at the surface, and I couldn't stop it. I start to panic and it happened. I had an anxiety attack right there in front of my toddler.

This is the point in the story where I wish I could tell you it didn't last long or that I had a quick way of coping to shut it down. But that didn't happen. My anxiety has looked different over the years, from anger to tears to full-blown panic attacks. That day, however, it was tears, which I consider my least traumatizing form of anxiety for others. I started to breathe heavily and the tears started to flow. I began to sob. While I don't remember much about the attack itself, I will never forget my daughter's face. Her expression transitioned from her own distress from having to get dressed and go to school, to shock and awe that mommy wasn't OK. Her mouth dropped and she looked at me confused with her deep blue eyes, trying to figure out what happened.

What occurred next brought me so much comfort and so much shame at the same time. My daughter embraced me. My toddler, who doesn't articulate that well and still runs and loses her balance, grabbed me and held me. She started stroking my arm and saying over and over "It's OK, mommy. It's going to be alright." The anxiety hadn't totally ended, and I was still sobbing, but I became so aware that my small child was calming me in a way that I couldn't do for myself. In an instant, I was both so proud that I was raising a nurturer while ashamed that she knew how to handle my anxiety better than I did in that moment.

However, simultaneously I realized I couldn't cope without help. I took in her words, felt her embrace and started to breathe through my tears. Gradually, my anxiety quelled, and I came back to my reality.

All the while knowing that my daughter not only witnessed this, but she helped me through it.

That day changed the way I see my anxiety. I work harder to employ coping skills as I see it bubbling. I am more consistent with my treatment and I employ my support system more frequently. However, it taught me a lot about parenting, too. While my daughter saw me in an undesirably vulnerable moment, she knew how to comfort. I taught her that. She knew the words to say without my prompting and knew to try and embrace me. I modeled that for her. Even though I don't wish for her to take care of me, I learned that I am raising a good human who models what I do and watches how I act. And as a parent with anxiety, I determine what she should know about my mental illness and how I set the example of resilience through it.

For someone who struggles with anxiety, there are a mix of emotions that I feel in the midst of an attack, especially around other people. I feel vulnerable, exposed, overwhelmed and pressured to get better quickly so no one knows how often and how intense my anxiety really is. But when it's my child, those feelings can be heightened because as a parent I believed the lie that I have to always be OK for her. The truth is, hiding my struggle with mental illness doesn't help her. It furthers the stigma that mental illness is wrong, bad and is a human flaw. Over the years, I've worked so hard to embrace my anxiety as part of who I am and how I cope is part of my strengths. When I hide this from her, I'm hiding part of me.

Do I need to show her all my anxiety? Absolutely not. Regardless of what age, I have to do my own work to take care of and parent her and continue to cope through my day. But I want her to know that I'm not always OK and that's a part of life for any person. I want her to see my use my coping skills whether it's generalized anxiety or if I happen to have an anxiety attack in her presence again. When I show her this, I'm giving her skills that can carry her through her own bad days, whether or not she has anxiety. Just like she knew to reassure me because I do that for her, how I overcome the tough things in life also teaches her how to keep going.

I know my first anxiety attack around her probably won't be the last. But what I learned from the first experience will shape the rest. My anxiety isn't just about me anymore, but it's about what I show her as she's watching me. While I hope my anxiety attacks in front of her are minimal, I hope she knows that her mom is not her mental illness. I want her to see my rise through the difficulty and see that anxiety won't stop me, but it will teach me something and make me stronger. And ultimately, I want her to learn that no matter what her tough days look like, she will rise too.

Mom's Not Okay

I laid on the couch for six hours. Six. As my husband tells my daughter to leave me alone, she approaches. She sees the pain in my eyes and begins to worry. At that moment she grabs my face and tells me, "It's okay mommy". I responded, "No it's not baby, but it will be". And in that moment, all I could do was cry.

Moments like these make me take stock of the struggle of depression and anxiety as an adult and as a parent. There are times in mothering that I have to remind myself that it's okay to not be okay. Living with mental illness is hard enough, but when you have a little one to parent you have to live with mental illness and live above it so they don't become your crutch. This is one of the most difficult things in life because I might not be okay, but I have to be.

My daughter does not take care of me, make me feel better, or is my anchor. She is my daughter and at the end of the day, I do know myself and the waves of my depression enough to know what I need. However, the moments that I need to just stay in bed or lay on the couch to take some time and heal are by far the hardest to do as a parent. I need those moments, but she sees sadness. I need to just be and no one to need anything from me, but she needs me. The push and pull to be okay and not feel okay is added stress and is a pain only mothers with mental illness will truly understand.

The pressure to be okay sometimes makes me more not okay. It forces me to move through my wave faster than I'm sometimes ready to handle. I have to know me and manage my mental illness so I can meet the needs of my child. And because I love her, I'm willing to do that. But as I manage it, she needs to know that sometimes being on the couch isn't all bad. Sometimes just being is healthy coping. Sometimes knowing that I'm not okay is honest and real It's better to live authentically, cope, and come through stronger. Mental illness shouldn't have a stigma because people with mental illness are people, survivors, warriors. I'm not okay, but I will be.

When She Looks at Me

She plays with reckless abandon. As she twirls in the field and picks flowers to give to everyone she sees, her heart is displayed on her sleeve because she loves and gives as far as her eye can see. She runs to me as if we've been apart for months, and she expresses how much she misses me and loves me. I love her hugs and kisses because they are genuine and never stem from obligation. She loves me and sees the beauty in me regardless of my day or my parenting. She wants to make me smile with her words and actions. She wants to love me and show me love.

As I look at her, I often remind myself of what I am not. I am too negative or skeptical, too busy and distracted. I look for the next thing to take on or to entertain me and can never stay in the moment. I want to please others but can't because I struggle to stay organized, to hold back my depression long enough to accomplish much. I don't want to be touched by others and I don't offer hugs as much as I used to. I don't play or twirl or pick flowers anymore. I am not her. However, I can learn from her.

She is the best of me. She reminds me that life is not all bad and it's not just one transaction to the next. When she looks at me with her big blue eyes and smiles, I melt. She is the light, and everything good in my world. In this moment I have a choice. I can choose now. I can choose to allow myself to be loved and love unconditionally. There is no need to please others, but there is a need to play and throw caution to the obligations that trap my daily distractions. I can choose to twirl and pick

When she looks at me with her big blue eyes and smiles, I melt. She is the light, and everything good in my world. My moments of darkness fade and I become who I want to be. I am free. I am fun. I am love.

Part 4: Surviving

Running and Coping

I recently ran a half-marathon. It was by far one of the hardest things I have done in my life, along with giving birth, breastfeeding and deciding to live through my darkest, most depressive moments. However, something unexpected happened. In the midst of trying to finish the race and post on social media in order to be praised for my accomplishments, I learned something about myself. I learned about how trying hard things impacts my mental health.

This race was like no other. I've run long distances before, and I've luckily never experienced bodily injury. Even though I had not run a half-marathon, I was confident it would be manageable, and I would come out on the other side sore but feeling great. That was not the case on this day. Before it began, I was excited, and the adrenaline was pumping as I crossed the starting line. The first mile was cold, but as my body warmed up. I felt alive. It was the rush that feels new and fresh with each run, and I knew the rest of this race was my time to shine. I didn't expect what was coming next.

A sharp pain behind my knee immediately coursed through my leg, giving me excruciating pain. I didn't understand why it was there. I stretched, I warmed up my body and I was ready. Why was this happening? I had previously gotten the advice from my sister-in-law to stretch every mile or walk at least 30 seconds at each marker, which I arrogantly thought was "crazy" until that point. But I was in pain, and I had to do something. With each mile, the pain increased. No amount of stretching or walking made it better. In fact, walking breaks had steadily made it worse. However, by mile six I was too far to turn back and all roads were closed for me to call for someone to pick me up.

I made it to mile eight before I was resolute that I needed to quit. I was determined to keep running in intervals to prove I was actually capable of *running* the half marathon. This stubborn view only cost me toward the end of the race. Then a beautiful thing happened. As I rounded the corner toward mile nine, there was my sister-in-law. She greeted with me cheers, smiles and a sign with my name on it. She had come out to the race for me and me alone, to let me know I could finish. In that moment, time froze. After I saw her, that was the moment I knew I could finish. It affirmed in my mind that I wasn't alone anymore, and even though she wasn't running with me, she was there to let me know I was capable of doing hard things.

The final miles were not only a blow to my ego but to my body. In the middle of mile 10, my body began to lock up. I started walking miles instead of seconds. At mile 12, I sobbed as I called my husband to tell me to keep going. At this point, he could have picked me up in the car and we could have gotten in the car without anyone knowing I didn't complete the half. Instead, he said, "you've done so many hard things in your life; make this one more."

He was right. While it was on the list of the hardest things — surviving suicide attempts, getting out of bed in the morning and reaching out to get the help I needed when I wanted to give up — were much harder first steps. This race was a reminder that when I'm at my weakest mentally or physically, I hadn't given up and it wasn't time to give up now. After that call, I began to run again. I saw the finish line and knowing that he and my family were at the end gave me a surge through my body that momentarily made me forget about the pain. And, as I crossed the finish line, Michelle Obama's words read to me through Audible came true: "at that moment it wasn't about anyone else, it was about me."

I completed the race that day. I took an hour longer than I planned, but it happened. I not only learned that I've done and can do hard things, but I am stronger than I remember most of the time. Even when plans go awry and life takes turns that take all we have to endure, it is possible to endure them. I, you, were made to endure, mental illness or not. And while continuing on may not take away the pain, it makes me stronger. With every obstacle, I become tougher and I learn something new about myself. I remember I've survived darkness to face the good and the bad of life. I've chosen to live, and part of that living is walking through every peak and valley in stride. Despite the long marathon of this life, the best part of facing new challenges is that I don't have to do them alone.

I invite people in my life who cheer me on and people to remind me of how far I've come. They cannot do what I do, or complete each obstacle for me, but my ability to ask for support and ask for what I need in the moment reflects my capability to keep moving. I have the power to challenge myself, to face the unexpected and complete each race. I am going to continue running, ready for the next finish line to cross.

Natural Disasters

Tornadoes, hurricanes, earthquakes, natural disasters all have an aftermath where the people affected by them have to assess the damage and start to rebuild. This year alone, I think I've experienced any and every disaster that I've been afraid to face. On top of that is depression which makes the recovery even harder.

I feel broken. The big events of grief, depression, change, friendships come and gone all rock my world that leaves me in a fight, flight or freeze. For every bad thing, there is some evidence of a natural disaster. And I'm left standing in the rubble.

At one point in time, I thought I was a strong person. I thought I could stand out in the middle of the rain and lightning and let the water hit my face with grace. But when the simple rain because a tsunami, I'm washed away. I thought I could change with the wind at any given moment, but when the earth starts to move faster than the wind, I'm too shaken. So when earth moved, the tsunami hit, I was found buried underneath everything.

I've gotten up since then. Every now and then some hail hits or a storm comes, but it's not like the tear down that happened in the past few months. So I look at he damage and try to understand it but I can't. It happened, it's over, but I have to clean it up. Where do I start? How do I clean up everything that's been destroyed and rebuild?

I really don't have the answers for this. All I know is that I can't live with torn down buildings and destroyed supplies. I have to rebuild. I have to find what hasn't been too far gone and try and salvage the left over pieces. And while that will be difficult, it must be done. Something needs to feel comfortable again.

The sky can't fall forever. Eventually, the aftershocks will subside and all the natural disasters in my life will move away. But today, it's about starting new again. I may be in the rubble but I'm a blank slate again. Start new, start over, find the sun again. I know it's there, I just need the clouds to clear for once. So here we go. It's time. I'm ready to pick up the pieces and start new. I just hope I'm done standing outside in the middle of a natural disaster.

Nature and Hope

I went outside today. And like most days, there is grass, trees, wind, and other living things that don't make me take a second look. But today I had a different look at the world outside, and I took a deep breath knowing what it all meant to me today.

There is grass. The grass starts out as dirt and fertilizer that is not pleasant to look at or something that is valued as something beautiful. Then it grows, and while it grows it acquires its color and becomes a luscious green. Even though that grass is taken for granted because sometimes it is viewed as just grass, if it were anything but grass, it would lose its value.

Next are the trees. The trees stand tall. They might be weathered and old, but the suffering they endure makes them ready for the next damage they face. They don't fall until they are cut down or are so badly damaged that they cannot stand anymore. And when they are cut, another tree can grow in its place, stronger than the one before. Trees grow new life. Whether it is used for survival or for aesthetic beauty, everything it grows is vital to its surroundings.

Then there is the wind. The wind guides everything that happens in nature because it is strong and forceful and yet doesn't hurt anything or take it out of its permanent place. The wind is so strong that it adds the most pleasure and can be a part of the most pain. The wind is beautiful in its silence, and strong in its presence. Even though it can't be seen, the feeling it brings lends itself to what is to come.

I saw a lot today. I saw everything new and nothing new at the same time. I was the grass. I was ugly made beautiful. In my growth I grew into my color and became a necessity to others in order to be seen and appreciated. I was the grass, knowing that without me, nothing else can be held up in the ground. I am the trees. I am weathered and worn and tired and I have rings of age. Sometimes events in my life try to cut me down, but nothing really makes me fall. Even if I did fall, I would spring up again. And most of all I grow life. With every relationship, with every student I teach, I speak life into that which I encounter. I am the trees because I refuse to let anything break me, and let everything make me grow and get stronger.

And finally, I will be the wind. One day, I will be so strong that whatever I do, it will be beautiful and powerful. I will never go away because my impact will one day never make anyone forget who I am. I will one day be effective and cause everything around me to move in a positive direction but never cause damage. In the future I will be beautiful in the silence, powerful in my presence, and unforgettable in my absence.

I went outside not realizing that I saw myself. I saw what I was, who I am, and who I can and will become. I went outside not meaning to discover everything that I did, but grateful that I know more coming back inside than I did before.

Broken but Mine

I met a woman many years ago. She's so beautiful and smart. When I first met her I knew she had something incredibly special about her. I was instantly drawn to her smile and her personality. She carries the weight of the world on her shoulders but walks as if she doesn't have a care in the world. She does so many things and is always determined to do and be more. She is my dream, and yet, her brokenness is a burden I bear.

Despite all that she is, she struggles. Some days she's on top of the world and checks everything off her list. But some days are so dark that a shower is her biggest accomplishment. Seeing her like this is so hard because no matter how hard I try, nothing helps. On the dark days, there's nothing I can do for her. I work to cheer her up, give her space, hold her close, call a friend for her, give her meds. Nothing. Where her mind goes is a mystery. It's almost as if life is too much so it goes blank. I feel helpless, but I made a vow to stay with her. And I will.

Depression cripples her, and anxiety makes her hate herself. When she's sad, there is no good. The pain radiates through the tears. She sleeps so long to forget the heaviness of her sickness. To ask her to function is too much. To ask her to return to normal can put her in a tailspin. When she's sick, I don't know what to do. I can only wait it out and hope she finds her way again.

I want to fix her so badly. I wish I knew a formula or a magic potion to help heal her. She is incredible and deserves to be whole. I know she wants to be whole, too. Neither of us know how to make that happen. But on her darkest days, she's not all she really is. She doesn't remember who she really is either. No matter what I do I can't remind her, because she doesn't believe me. It's like she can't hear me.

No matter what, I'm committed to her. My love for her, our family, our life, will see us through. The good days far outweigh the bad, because I see her true worth. Regardless of the dark times, I choose to stay. I choose her. Dark or light, there's always a twinkle in her eye. I made a vow in sickness and in health, and she's worth both.

Today and every day I choose her. I choose to keep fighting, keep trying, keep nursing her back to health. I love her for who she is even when she can't show it. She chooses to stay for both of us. She is resilient and pushes through. She may be broken, but it is what makes her her. She is worthy of my love and worth fighting for. She is mine.

She is me.

Mental Health Resources

Apps for Coping:

- Calm
- Headspace
- My 3
- What's Up
- MindShift
- Emoods
- Happify
- Rise Up and Recover
- nOCD
- Breathe to Relax

Therapy Listing Sites:

- Psychologytoday.com

- Therapyforblackgirls.com

- Inclusivetherapists.com

- Openpathcollective.com

- Melaninandmentalhealth.com

- Postpartum.net

- Therapyforqpoc.com